"I wish I had thought more about growing older when I was younger. If I had, perhaps I wouldn't need wisdom from J. I. Packer. But I didn't, and therefore I do! And what wonderful wisdom it is, the sort that challenges us, redirects our energy, and equips us with biblical truth to face our latter years. I'm at that stage in life where 'engaging' with my 'aging' has become increasingly more urgent. And I can't think of anyone who can provide more helpful and encouraging insight than J. I. Packer. Don't wait until you're sixty or seventy to read this book. Start now and finish well."

Sam Storms, Senior Pastor, Bridgeway Church, Oklahoma City, Oklahoma

"J. I. Packer is his usual wise self as he gives his counsel herein for older people to pursue their aging with 'zeal'! He urges us to serve God and his church however we can, while we can. This is devout and inspiring motivation."

Marva J. Dawn, theologian; speaker; author, *Being Well When We're Ill*; *In the Beginning, GOD*; and *Talking the Walk*

"Experts say that the proportion of the elderly population in the United States will grow by 80 percent in the decades to come. It is more important than ever to have a biblical mind about how we spend our latter years for God's glory. We want to finish well (2 Tim. 4:7), and good pastors care to prepare their people to do precisely this. *Finishing Our Course with Joy* comes as wise, true, timely, and edifying biblical reflection and pastoral counsel on this significant subject. Dr. Packer's book speaks to senior adults, those who love and care for them, those who will become them, and those who pastor them. As one who has had the privilege of knowing J. I. Packer since my teen years, reading these words—written from his own personal experience, communion with God, and knowledge of the Word—is poignant for me, to say the least. But that only makes the truth go in deeper. And that is good."

J. Ligon Duncan III, Chancellor and
John E. Richards Professor of Systematic
and Historical Theology, Reformed Theological
Seminary, Jackson, Mississippi

Finishing
Our Course
with Joy

Other Crossway Books by J. I. Packer

A Grief Sanctified: Through Sorrow to Eternal Hope

Growing in Christ

Praying the Lord's Prayer

Keeping the Ten Commandments

In My Place Condemned He Stood: Celebrating the Glory of the Atonement (with Mark Dever)

Affirming the Apostles' Creed

A Quest for Godliness: The Puritan Vision of the Christian Life

Faithfulness and Holiness: The Witness of J. C. Ryle

Taking God Seriously: Vital Things We Need to Know

Weakness Is the Way: Life with Christ Our Strength

FINISHING
OUR COURSE
WITH JOY

Guidance from God
for Engaging with Our Aging

J. I. PACKER

WHEATON, ILLINOIS

First printing 2014
Printed in the United States of America

Scripture quotations are from the ESV® Bible (*The Holy Bible, English Standard Version*®), copyright © 2001 by Crossway. 2011 Text Edition. Used by permission. All rights reserved.

Trade paperback ISBN: 978-1-4335-4106-3
PDF ISBN: 978-1-4335-4107-0
Mobipocket ISBN: 978-1-4335-4108-7
ePub ISBN: 978-1-4335-4109-4

Library of Congress Cataloging-in-Publication Data
Packer, J. I. (James Innell)
   Finishing our course with joy : guidance from God for engaging with our aging / J. I. Packer.
      pages cm
   Includes index.
   ISBN 978-1-4335-4106-3
   1. Older people—Religious life. 2. Aging—Religious aspects—Christianity. I. Title.
BV4580.P235   2014
248.8'5—dc23   2013026732

Crossway is a publishing ministry of Good News Publishers.

VP   26   25   24   23   22   21
15   14   13   12   11   10   9   8

To Jim Houston
in gratitude

Contents

1

We Grow Old

Four days in June 2012 were set apart for celebrating the diamond jubilee of Europe's veteran monarch, Her Britannic Majesty Elizabeth II, Queen of the United Kingdom and the British Commonwealth. I, who am British by birth and Canadian by choice, resonated with the celebration and on day four, began to pen this book.

It addresses those who, like myself, are well into aging. Nowadays, we elderlies (as I have heard us called) are classified as younger olds (65–75), medium olds (75–85), and oldest olds (85 plus). Queen Elizabeth, like her husband, is an oldest old; she is 87, he is 92.

The Queen is a very remarkable person. Tirelessly, it seems, she goes on doing what she has been doing for six decades and more: waving in shy friendliness to the crowds past whom she is transported, and greeting with a smile one and another, children particularly, whom she meets in her walkabouts. It is more than sixty years since she publicly committed herself before God to serve Commonwealth citizens all her life. She has done it devotedly up to now, and will undoubtedly continue doing it as long as she physically can. So we may expect to see more of the porkpie hats and hear more of the clear, easy voice as her reign continues. She is a Christian lady resolved to live out her vow till she drops. She merits unbounded admiration from us all.

As myself a Christian, a Commonwealth citizen, and an oldest old with my own lifetime commitment to God, I aim to follow her example of unflagging faithfulness, and I write these pages in hope of persuading others to do the same.

As I write, I am aware that some of my peers will not be fully with me at this point; not because their Christian commitment is less strong than mine, but because they are now limited in what they can think and do by reason of their physical health breaking down or, more sadly, some form of dementia, that is, impaired working of the mind due to malfunction of the brain. For us in the oldest-old class, these things are usually irreversible.

It is true that modern medicine and surgery keep our bodies going longer, and some think it will be possible to extend ordinary people's bodily lives to something like 120 years. Yet who would choose that prospect if they thought that for up to half a century, certainly more than a third of their extended life, they would be victims of dementia? This is a possibility that can hardly be ruled out, for already one in four of us oldest old experience dementia in some form, and clearly the odds will shorten the longer our lives last.

Be that as it may, these pages address those who, by God's grace, still have their faculties more or less intact; who recognize that, as is often and truly said, aging is not for wimps; and who want to learn, in a straightforward way, how we may continue living to God's glory as we get older.

DECLINE

How should we view the onset of old age? The common assumption is that it is mainly a process of loss, whereby strength is drained from both mind and body and the capacity to look forward and move forward in life's various departments is reduced to nothing. More than four centuries ago, Shakespeare put this assessment into the mouth of the melancholy Jaques in *As You Like It*. Surveying the seven ages of man on the world stage, Jaques comes to this:

> Last scene of all
> That ends this strange eventful history
> Is second childishness and mere
>   oblivion;
> Sans teeth, sans eyes, sans taste, sans
>   everything.
>
>   (act 2, scene 7)

And in the Bible, two thousand years or more before Shakespeare, Ecclesiastes, the preacher-teacher-philosopher-wiseacre-pundit, not so much a pessimist as a realist who depicts everything as it appears "under the sun" to the thoughtful observer, urges the young to "remember . . . your Creator in the days of your youth, before the evil days come . . . ; before the sun and the light and the moon and the stars are darkened" (joy in being alive fades), "and the clouds return after the rain" (troubles recur), "in the day when the keepers of the house tremble" (arms weaken, hands shake), "and the strong men" (legs) "are bent, and the grinders" (teeth) "cease because they are few" (they drop out), "and those who look through the windows" (eyes) "are dimmed, and the doors on the street are shut" (deafness develops)— "when the sound of the grinders is low" (chewing becomes an effort), "and one rises up at the sound of a bird" (sudden small noises, however sweet, upset one), "and all the daughters of song are brought low" (music, from being a delight, becomes a bore)—"they are afraid also of what is high" (balance goes, dizziness comes), "and terrors are in the way" (one frequently feels frightened); "the almond tree blossoms" (hair turns white), "the grasshopper drags itself along" (one's walking grows erratic and un-steady), "and desire fails" (emotional numb-ness sets in) . . . (Eccles. 12:1–5).

The picture is of loss, weakness, and apa-thy, leading to death. That is Ecclesiastes's story about aging.

RIPENESS

But neither in the Bible nor in life is this the whole story. Listen again to Shake-speare. In his tragedy *King Lear*, one of the world's classics on dysfunctional families, a dispossessed son who refuses to be embit-tered by the way he has been treated com-ments thus on his blinded father's loss of the will to live:

> Men must endure
> Their going hence, even as their coming hither;
> Ripeness is all.

> (act 5, scene 2)

"Ripeness"—what does that mean? The word carries the very positive meaning of maturity, corresponding to the ripeness of fruit. We know the difference between ripe and unripe fruit: the latter is sharp, acid, hard, without much flavor, and sets teeth on edge; the former is relatively soft and sweet, juicy, mellow, flavorful, leaving a pleasant aftertaste in the mouth.

Between human beings in and beyond middle age a comparable difference appears. Some grow old gracefully, meaning, fully in the grip of the grace of God. Increasingly they display a well-developed understanding with a well-formed character: firm, resilient, and unyielding, with an unfailing sense of proportion and abundant resources for upholding and mentoring others. In Shakespeare's play, however, "Ripeness is all" should be said with a certain gloominess, for the thought being expressed is that this personal ripeness will again and again be all that one has at the end of life, though one expected, and had a right to expect, much more.

But here the Bible breaks in, highlighting the further thought that spiritual ripeness is worth far more than material wealth in any form, and that spiritual ripeness should continue to increase as one gets older.

The Bible's view is that aging, under God and by grace, will bring wisdom, that is, an enlarged capacity for discerning, choosing, and encouraging. In Proverbs 1–7 an evidently elderly father teaches realistic moral and spiritual wisdom to his adult but immature son. In Psalm 71 an elderly preacher who has given the best years of his life to teaching the truth about God in the face of much opposition prays as follows:

> You, O LORD, are my hope,
>   my trust, O LORD, from my youth. . . .

Do not cast me off in the time of
    old age;
  forsake me not when my strength is
    spent. . . .

But I will hope continually
  and will praise you yet more and
    more.
My mouth will tell of your
    righteous acts,
  of your deeds of salvation all the day,
  for their number is past my
    knowledge.
With the mighty deeds of the Lord God
    I will come;
  I will remind them of your
    righteousness, yours alone.

O God, from my youth you have
    taught me,
  and I still proclaim your wondrous
    deeds.
So even to old age and gray hairs,
  O God, do not forsake me,

until I proclaim your might to another
generation,
your power to all those to come.
(Ps. 71:5, 9, 14–18)

And Psalm 92:12 and 14 declare:

The righteous flourish like the palm tree
and grow like a cedar in Lebanon. . . .
They still bear fruit in old age;
they are ever full of sap and green.

LAST LAP

This biblical expectation and, indeed, promise of ripeness growing and service of others continuing as we age with God is the substance of the last-lap image of our closing years, in which we finish our course. Runners in a distance race, like jockeys in a horse race, always try to keep something in reserve for a final sprint. And my contention is going to be that, so far as our bodily health allows, we should aim to be found running the last lap of the race of our Christian life, as we would say, flat out. The final sprint, so I urge, should be a sprint indeed.

"Live each day as if thy last" is a wise word from a hymn written in 1674 by Thomas Ken. The older we get, the more needful its wisdom becomes, and if we have not already taken it to heart, we should do so now. When we unpack Ken's admonition, three thoughts emerge.

First, *live for God one day at a time*. Whatever long-term plans we may have, we need to get into the habit of planning each day's business in advance, either first thing each morning or (better, I think) the day before. Glorifying God should be our constant goal, and to that end we need to acquire the further habit of reviewing before God as each day closes how far we have done as we planned, or whether and why and how far we changed the plan to fit new circumstances and fresh insights, and in any case how far we did the best we could for our God, and how far we fell short of doing that. Surely it is increasingly important that we be doing this as we approach the end of life and the prospect of giving an account of ourselves to God.

Second, *live in the present moment.* Get into the way of practicing God's presence—more specifically, Christ's presence, according to his promise to be with us always (Matt. 28:20)—and cultivate the divine companionship. This, too, is an important and, I suspect, widely neglected spiritual discipline nowadays, and its importance also would seem to grow as we near life's end.

Daydreaming and indulgence of nostalgia are unhappy habits, making for unrealism and discontent. Like all bad habits, they tighten their grip on us until we set ourselves against them and, with God's help, break them. Elderly retirees are prone to find that a disciplined breaking of them is an increasingly necessary task in life's last lap, in which steady looking ahead in each present moment becomes a bigger and bigger factor in inner spiritual health.

Third, *live ready to go when Christ comes for you.* Jesus's words to the faithful eleven are in fact a promise to all his faithful disciples in every age:

> In my Father's house are many rooms. If it were not so, would I have told you that I go to prepare a place for you? And if I go and prepare a place for you, I will come again and will take you to myself, that where I am you may be also. (John 14:2–3)

The experience of dying varies from one to another. Some of us will be conscious and relatively alert right up to the moment of our going; some will sink into unconsciousness as our bodies progressively close down; some will die in a coma, or while asleep, or in a sudden accident or attack on our person, or from heart stoppage; and we cannot foresee how it will be for us. So the way of wisdom is to be ready for whatever comes, whenever it comes.

What does this involve? More than merely making a will, giving directions for one's funeral, and arranging for the disposal of one's property. First and foremost, it involves direct, sober dealing with the Lord Jesus Christ himself, who is not only the one who will come as our courier to take us through our transition from this world to the next, but also the one who at some point in that world will be our Judge. "For we must all appear before the judgment seat of Christ, so that each one may receive what is due for what he has done in the body, whether good or evil" (2 Cor. 5:10). More about that later; here, I would only stress the urgency of entering, here and now, by faith, into a personal relation of discipleship to Christ, the invisibly present Savior and Lord, as in and through the gospel he himself invites everyone to do. This will banish all fears about our future.

A British professor of theology once described to me the world to which believers will go as "an unknown country with a well-known inhabitant." When Jesus Christ the courier has already become well known to us through the Gospels and Pastoral Letters of the New Testament, the prospect of transitioning with him into a world in which we shall see him as he is and be constantly in his company will be something we find alluring rather than alarming.

WRONG WAY

But now we must face the fact that all forms of this ideal of ripeness and increased focus in life in our old age stand in direct contrast to the advice for old age that our secular Western world currently gives. Retirees are admonished, both explicitly and implicitly, in terms that boil down to this: Relax. Slow down. Take it easy. Amuse yourself. Do only what you enjoy.

You are not required to run things anymore, or to exercise any form of creativity, or to take responsibility for guiding and sustaining goal-oriented enterprises. You are off the treadmill and out of the rat race. Now, at last, you are your own man (or woman) and can concentrate on having fun. You have your pension; health services are there to look after your body; and clubs, trips, outings, tours, competitions, games, parties, and entertainments are provided in abundance to help you pass the time.

So now go ahead and practice self-indulgence up to the limit. Fill your life with novelties and hobbies, anything and everything that will hold your interest. As far as society is concerned, you are now on the shelf; you have only yourself, with or without your spouse, to please and look after and worry about, so concentrate on that; and live as if your life of retirement, with enough health and strength for daily functioning, will go on forever, being constantly lengthened by modern medical magic. You are entitled to be cared for as long as your life can be made to last; so make the most of it! If your old age is dreary and boring, it will be entirely your own fault, and you don't want that.

Road signs reading "Wrong Way" tell us that if we press forward, we shall find ourselves going against the traffic in a one-way street or following a road that peters out, leads nowhere, or has become impassable. Such signs are usually preceded by other signs indicating the right way to go. The phrase "Wrong Way" is a blunt verbal instrument, waking us up to the fact that we are ignoring something—missing it, as we would say. And that is just what I affirm with regard to our culture's agenda for aging. I think it is one of the huge follies of our time, about which some frank speaking is in order and indeed overdue. I ask you to bear with me now as I share what I see with regard to the advice that I crystallized in the preceding paragraphs.

I see this agenda, well meant as it is, as wrongheaded in the extreme. I think it is ironically deceptive, calculated in effect to produce the precise opposite of the fullness of elderly life that it purports to promote. What is wrong with it? For the moment I leave aside its lack of Christian content and focus on the fact that it prescribes idleness, self-indulgence, and irresponsibility as the goal of one's declining years. This, over time, will generate a burdensome sense that one's life is no longer significant, but has become, quite simply, useless.

The experience of no longer working with colleagues in a team to achieve some worthwhile result is likely to bring on loneliness, restlessness, and depression. Having nothing of importance to look forward to will certainly breed a discontented narcissism, probably accompanied by a sustained displeasure at the way things are and an ongoing sense that one has a right to be better looked after than is currently the case. The fact that one is no longer under any pressure to use one's mind in learning things, solving problems, or strategizing for benefits either to oneself or to anybody else, will allow intelligence to lie permanently fallow, and this, so they tell us, may very well hasten the onset of dementia. The agenda as a whole turns out to be a recipe for isolating oneself and trivializing one's life, with apathetic boredom becoming one's default mood day after day.

In my early years, one of my grandmothers lived with us in our home. When I recall the setup, I wince. She was, as far as I know, in fair health for a medium old. Daily she stayed in her room, eating breakfast and lunch off trays we took up to her, until evening mealtime drew near. She would then come downstairs and eat with us, after which she would sit in her chair and watch what we were doing, speaking when spoken to but not otherwise, until bedtime. Did she read the paper? I cannot recall, but she certainly read no books while she was downstairs. She left the house only once or twice a year, when a distant relative with a car would come and take her for a drive. Otherwise she remained housebound. She died at eighty-five, when I was eight.

Today I wonder whether she was depressed during those years, when we effectively excluded her from the to-ing and fro-ing of family life and thus, I imagine, made her feel she did not count as a member of the family itself. It is a bad memory that haunts me as I think about seniors in nuclear families today.

In my view, on which I shall say a bit more later, any ideology or social blueprint or behavior pattern that has the effect of detaching the elderly from the ongoing life of what today we call the nuclear family is misguided and inappropriate. But before we go further with that, I need to make some additional points about aging in general.

2

Soul and Body

To see how we should live, we need first and foremost to know who and what we are. This is true throughout our lives, but particularly is it so as we grow old and are tempted, as we say, to not "be (or act) our age"—that is, to think and behave as if we are still what we were years back, and so to not come to terms with how we have changed and what has become true of us today. As we shall see, this temptation is widespread and strong, and there is a reason for that. But some basic things must be clarified before that topic can be taken up.

EMBODIED SOULS, ENSOULED BODIES

Where then should we start in seeking realistic, up-to-date, present-tense self-knowledge as we age? Experience from infancy onward convinces us, when we think about it, that we are in some sense bipartite. That is, we are personal selves living in and through physical bodies, on which we depend for energy and ability to do things according to our desires, and by which we are limited, kept from doing much that we would like to be able to do. These physical bodies of ours face us again and again with the need to do things—sleep, eat, urinate, defecate, and so on—which, at least on occasion, we wish we did not need to do. But in these things we have to be their servants, just as in other things we make them ours.

Our bodies can be taught physical skills, though brainwork must accompany the dexterity in each case (think of sports skills, surgical skills, driving and piloting skills, for example); similarly, our souls can learn mental skills like logic and mathematics; and there are skills, like musical performance, in which soul and body combine. Understandably and insightfully, today's Christian thinkers tell us that we should think of ourselves as embodied souls that are also ensouled bodies, and should regard the soul and the body as distinct but inseparable, bonded together in a whole series of ways, from birth to death.

But what then? To this question different answers are given. Centuries before Christ, the Greek philosopher Plato guessed that our embodiment is a limitation on our growth; that our bodies are like prisons and tombs, where our souls, the real persons that we are, are confined till the day the body expires. But then the soul leaves the body behind and flies away into a realm of reality where goodness, truth, and beauty, life's supreme glories, can be known and lived with in a way that was not possible before. Many since Plato, and often quite independently of him, have embraced this idea in some form and cherished the notion that happiness is ultimately increased by being set free from our bodies—as if being embodied keeps us from fullness of life, joy, knowledge, contentment, and whatever else we feel at different stages of our existence that we never have enough of.

Christians, however, disagree. Guided by Scripture, their faith is focused on (1) the incarnation of the Son of God, whereby the second person of the Trinity took to himself all that is involved in being human, living through a body included, and (2) the resurrection of Jesus into an unending life of which his glorified humanity is a permanent part. Now they look forward to their own coming enrichment through the resurrection of their own bodies, significantly renewed and transformed as their souls too will have been. They anticipate being reimplanted in those transformed bodies and reinhabiting them to all eternity in a re-created order of reality. There they will grow, advance, bloom, and find delight in all sorts of ways through the ever-deepening communion of their flawlessly renovated personal being with Jesus Christ, their divine Savior, their Lord, and their friend. The eternal re-embodiment of their souls will, they believe, be integral to this life of glory.

It is certainly the case that as Christians age they sometimes feel that, for whatever specific reason—exhaustion, starvation, disease, irreparable structural damage to their physical system, irreversible degenerative malfunctioning within that system, and so forth—their bodies have become burdensome and restrictive to their souls, keeping them from doing and enjoying what they would be doing and enjoying were it not for their physical troubles. But to conclude from this that one's soul—the thinking, feeling, remembering, imagining, communicating self that one is—would be freer and happier separated from one's body than it ever can be otherwise would be a grave mistake. God's plan for us is different, as we shall now see.

It will help us forward if the basic questions about bodies and souls in God's revealed purpose for us are now laid out and responded to in order. Here they are.

What Are Human Beings, and Why Did God Invent Us?

All members of the human race are psychophysical units, embodied souls who are also ensouled bodies, as we have seen already. Mankind (originally, a single pair to whom God gave a procreative agenda—Gen. 1:28) was made to manage the ordered environment that God had created for his own pleasure. And with that we were to find pleasure of our own in giving God the glory of our human praise and thanks and service.

When, unhappily, sin, the defiant disregard of God and his will, corrupted human nature, as it did right at the start of the human story, God initiated a plan of redemptive restoration through Jesus Christ for the fulfilling of his original purpose in a re-created cosmic frame, and that is what humanity is involved with now. Not all human individuals actually share in this restoration; those who do are those who, confronted by the gospel, put faith in Jesus and become his disciples.

God seems always to have intended that the life of humans in this world should be probationary and temporary, and should lead in due course to some form of transformation and transition for a richer life elsewhere. And death as we know it, with discernible physical decline ordinarily preceding it, is no part of God's good creation, but is his judgment on sin, as Genesis 3 declares.

What Are Our Souls?

The human soul, as was indicated above, is the conscious personal self, the "I" that knows itself as "me," the built-in principle of awareness, responsiveness, interaction, and relationships. Cognitive enquiry and thought; interrogation of persons, situations, and resources; memory of things past and the sense of identity that remembering generates; feeling emotions and forming plans; perceiving and performing creative work in the arts, and grasping the reality of goodness, beauty, and truth; creative relationships with other people—all these and more are activities of our souls or, as we may prefer to say, our hearts. (In Scripture "soul" and "heart" both refer to the central core of personhood that is the inward source of all our behavior and reactions, and the words are almost identical in meaning.) Soul life will continue when physical life—body life, as we may call it—has ceased. Indeed, the personal self-awareness that is ours now will never cease, but will be enhanced and extended, for sorrow or for joy, through all eternity.

What Is the Purpose of Our Bodies?

It seems clear that God gave us bodies to live in and through for two reasons: first, to fit us for managing the material world of which we are made his trustees and stewards; and, second, to enrich our lives here and now. Bodies are demonstrably given us for experience, expression, and enjoyment:

- *Experience.* Think of all that comes to us through our five physical senses, and through our various body-based sensations, and through our reactions, pro and con, to the people and things we encounter.
- *Expression.* Think of all that is communicated by the looks on people's faces, including our own; the way folk stand in front of you, cuddle up to you, draw away from you, and so forth.
- *Enjoyment.* Think of the pleasures that are given us through eating, drinking, smelling, listening to music, lying in bed, winning in a physical sport, or relaxing after hard work.

These are samples only; the list could be extended. William Temple said, "God likes matter—he made it." We may equally say, "God likes pleasures—he devised them." A moment's thought makes it obvious that life without a body would be greatly impoverished.

TENSION AND TEMPTATION

But bodies wear out, and that is what we have to come to terms with as we age.

Until we are about sixty-five, or are getting on that way, most of us are likely to feel that our bodies and our souls (or, since "soul" is an antiquated word outside the church, we may choose to say "minds" or "brain cells" or "marbles") are keeping up with each other pretty well. We are living comfortably with ourselves; we know what we can and cannot tackle mentally and physically, and we have long since ceased to fret, as perhaps we did in adolescence, at not being able to do all sorts of things we would like to do, but realize are beyond us.

Now, however, in our sixties, we find ourselves facing new limitations. We cannot do this and that as easily as once we could. Energy level shrinks; memory is not what it was; aches, pains, and shortness of breath become permanent facts of life; we tire more quickly; bones break more easily. Our bodies are wearing out, as all human bodies have done since Adam fell and God pronounced the death sentence on him. They will go on wearing out as long as we live. Exercise, medication, and careful dieting may slow down the process, but they will not reverse it.

John Wesley at eighty-five wrote in his journal that the only sign of deterioration that he could see in himself was that he could not run as fast as he used to. With all due deference to that wonderful, seemingly tireless little man, we may reasonably suspect that he was overlooking some things at this point, just as some do when they assure us that they never had a day's illness in their life. We cannot stop our bodies aging, any more than King Canute's say-so could stop the tide coming in.

Furthermore, as our bodies wear out,

they become more vulnerable to infections, breakdowns, heart problems, and cancers. Down syndrome and schizophrenia do not vanish with age, and forms of dementia, such as Alzheimer's disease, are apt to develop. The slowing down is permanent, and with it comes one of the two temptations that are peculiar to old age—namely, to go with the flow of bodily decline and waning physical desires, and to allow our discipleship to Christ and our zeal for seeking, displaying, and advancing the kingdom of God also to slow down, or maybe I should say cool down, in a way that corresponds. This, however, is a big topic and calls for a chapter to itself.

Meantime, however, think back with me for a moment to the oldsters' temptation that I referred to at the start of this chapter, namely, not facing up to the fact that our physical decline is actually happening. Why this obstinate unrealism? The answer is not far to seek. Behind this attitude stands pride—pride, the essence of original sin as Augustine diagnosed it; pride, the irrational, insatiable drive always to be the one on top and in charge, always honoring, serving, and pleasing the great god self; pride, that treats domination, control, and outscoring rivals as a never-ending task.

Those who have had successful careers are often in dominant positions when old age sets in, retirement becomes due, and bowing out is the appropriate action, and it should cause no surprise when they resist the prospect and try to evade or at least postpone it. Nor should it surprise us when such persons, having reluctantly left the field of what they saw as their former fulfillment, become tyrannical in their own family and among their own friends in a way that they never were before.

Proverbial Christian wisdom, backed by the Bible itself, tells us that we all face temptations from three sources: the world (circumstances and conditions surrounding us), the flesh (prideful original sin within us—the reality about which we have just been speaking—constantly generating attitudes of what we may call un-love), and the Devil (a malevolent intelligence riding herd on us and orchestrating the attacks of both pridefulness and worldliness against us). Frank acknowledgment of these sorts of temptation, and of Satan's interest in each, is needed as we seek to plot the proper path for godly aging.

3

Keeping Going

I was still in junior high school, as I recall, when a teacher told me that the secret of effective writing is to know your ideal reader. It seems to me that for more than half a century I have been proving the truth of his words, and I am sure it will help us forward at this stage if now I say something more about my ideal readers than I have said thus far. So let me turn my telescope on them and be as explicit about them as I can.

The readers whom I am addressing, as I indicated at the outset, are Christian seniors in or near my own age group. They became Christians in youth or early middle age and have been believers for several decades. They appreciate that learning to live with one's old age is a spiritual discipline in itself, and they are reading this book in hope that it might help them there. Throughout this chapter, in which I shall state in some detail what I am assuming about them, I shall address them as "you."

SENIOR BELIEVERS IN PROFILE

You Became Christians

You were not born Christian in any substantive sense; no one is. Each Christian in this world is a person who intentionally became one, as people intentionally become engineers or electricians. Maybe you had a conversion experience of some kind, in which you found yourself reckoning with the reality of the Lord Jesus Christ within a frame of crisis, choice, and decision. You became aware of his presence accompanying you and confronting you. You thanked him because he died for your sins, and you ceased to defy his claims on you. You trusted him as your Savior, gave yourself to him as your Lord and leader, and embraced him as your guardian, guide, and friend. You repented of particular transgressions, and resolved to live henceforth as his disciple, loving and obeying him as best you could. You committed yourself to daily devotional procedures (systematic Bible reading, a particular pattern of prayer, or whatever your routine was). You remember when this took place, and you could give the date of it if there were need.

Or maybe the coming of your present convictions about Christ, and your current commitment to him, was a gradual process over a period of time, about which all you can say for sure is that it certainly happened, and now you are a different person inside from what you once were, and what others whom you know well still are. But happen it did, and for decades now you have been practicing Christ's presence, basking in the truth of his promise to be with you always, at all times, and in all circumstances (Matt. 28:20), while you yourself engage, more or less deeply, in the routines that in recent years have been singled out as the distinctive disciplines of the Christian life: Bible reading with meditation, prayer with praise, journaling with self-examination, corporate worship and fellowship, reading and learning, spells of silence and solitude.

You Have Served Christ

I see you as veterans of the war between the forces of Christ and those of Satan. From the start you knew that you were saved to serve, and that indeed is what you spontaneously wanted to do. Soon you learned, however, that you were going to be opposed all the way. By becoming Christians you walked into a war, Satan's war against the triune God, the Father, the Son, and the Holy Spirit. And that meant that whatever you set yourselves to do by way of service to your Lord, satanic forces would try, usually by indirect rather than direct means, to thwart or spoil. So your Christian life has been a long-drawn fight against the world, the flesh, and the Devil, and such it still is.

Nonetheless, you have lived full and varied lives. You married and brought up families, doing your best to nurture them in Christian faith. Following the lead of your circumstances, and of your abilities, and of the interests God has put in your hearts, you carved out careers for yourselves. Also, you joined local churches, where you sought to pull your weight as helpers, encouragers, givers, teachers, counselors, and friends. You sought to support the lonely and to stabilize those who in any way were feeling life's strain and battling despair. You used your home for hospitality and group gatherings, and you kept your eyes and ears open for opportunities to share your faith.

Some of you were church officers, pastors even; maybe you invested yourself in parachurch ministries, reaching out for Christ in a way that the established congregations were unable to do. You labored to live intensely for Jesus in each present moment, asking him constantly in your heart, "Lord, what is the best I can do/say/give/take on for your kingdom and your glory, placed as I am right now?"—and you have known the gift of wise insight in answer to that prayer.

Such, then, has been your track record in serving Christ up to the present. You have lived, loved, and labored for him, not always with great success, but with constant faithfulness and zeal. Your faith has shown its genuineness by the good works achieved and the battles fought. Yes, you are veterans indeed.

You Sought Holiness

Each of you knows, as all real Christians do, that God's grace finds us in a state of radical unholiness, which it calls on us to change. You know that God, who reconciled us to himself through the death of his Son, and justified us through faith, and adopted us as children in his family, now commands us to be holy because he is holy himself. You know that positionally and relationally we become holy through separation, consecration, and being set apart to God and for God, while in personal and subjective terms our holiness is a supernaturalized way of life in which obedience, love, praise, and the practice of visionary, God-honoring righteousness all flow from our purified hearts through the power of the Holy Spirit.

Knowing all this, and desiring its fullest

fulfillment in your life, you set your face against the many forms of immorality, inhumanity, and dishonesty with which our culture surrounds us, and you worked hard both to keep yourself from acts of sin, expressing pride and self-will, and to keep at bay dreams of sin, which when welcomed befoul the heart, even though they are not acted out. You cultivated a sensitivity of conscience with regard to sin and formed a habit of watching and praying against it.

Knowing yourself to be a new creation in Christ, united to and bonded with him by the indwelling Holy Spirit, you rejoice to think that the flesh—that is, indwelling sin, the sum and substance of all our skewed, self-serving inclinations—is no longer the dominant driving force in your life that it once was. Yet you have to admit that it is still there, operating in its deceitful and destructive way as a kind of satanic second self, dragging us down into at least the thought-world of misbehavior, even if not the actuality of sinning outright.

Again and again you have resisted the pull and the pressure of indwelling sin, and when at times you realized you had slipped spiritually (and who has not slipped on occasion?), you sought and found repentance, forgiveness, and recovery. So your years-long purpose of pleasing God daily remains intact as now you move into and through old age.

It is with this profile of you in my mind that I go on to say what I have to say about the distinctive temptation that we find raising its head against us all in our old age.

SENIOR BELIEVERS UNDERMINED

In the Bible, temptations are tests in which we are tried out, as the world would express it, to see what we are made of: what resources of wisdom, thoughtfulness, watchfulness, discernment, humility, consistency, trust, faithfulness, hope, and inward stability and strength are there in us to be drawn on when we are put under pressure.

The Devil and God both test us in this fashion. Satan and his minions do it in order to bring us down in flames, as Satan brought down Eve and Adam in Eden and tried to bring down Job in the land of Uz, and to bring down Jesus in the desert. By contrast, God does it as a training exercise, to strengthen his servants for their future role in his plans, as when he required Abraham to show himself willing to sacrifice his son Isaac (Genesis 22), and when he permitted Satan to ruin Job's life (Job 1–2), and when the Holy Spirit drove Jesus into the desert to undergo Satan's temptations (Mark 1:12–13). Much here is hidden from us, but from time to time, in the same event, we can see both Satan's malice in the foreground and the gracious purpose of God's overruling providence in the background. Certainly, when Satan tempts, God is always present, just as when God blesses, Satan is never absent.

All we who are Christians are repeatedly put under temptation one way or another (C. S. Lewis's classic *Screwtape Letters* will enlarge your insight into this), and the temptation always operates at a point where Satan sees us to be vulnerable. So we need to be constantly on our guard, for Satan's first move whenever he tempts is to persuade us, one way or another, to lower our guard and for the moment forget that near us is a cunning Enemy who will bring us to spiritual ruin if he can. The revived emphasis on spiritual warfare in recent times, though not always well conceived and applied, was needed, and still is, not least by us seniors; for Satan's war against each of us will end only with the end of this present life.

Luke records that Jesus, just before his betrayal, spoke to his disciples as "you . . .

who have stayed with me in my trials" (Luke 22:28; the Greek word for "temptations" is used here). These words link up with Luke's observation that following his threefold failure in the desert the tempter left Jesus "until an opportune time" (4:13)—opportune, that is, for renewing his attempts to divert Jesus from his Father's plan: that he become the sin-bearing sacrifice by which sinners would be saved. When Peter, out of mistaken expectations and misguided good-will, tried similarly to divert Jesus from embracing the cross, Jesus responded, "Get behind me, *Satan!*" (Matt. 16:23)—for he saw that Satan was using Peter as his mouthpiece at this point. Getting Jesus to evade the cross was, as it would seem, the focus of Satan's temptation during the years of Jesus's ministry. And this leads on to the specific temptation by which Christ's elderly disciples are nowadays assailed.

That temptation is one form of an allurement we have all been exposed to since our Christian lives began, namely, to conform without thinking to what is already taking place. We go with the flow, following the path that the secular community (and often too the institutional church to which we belong) is on already; and we identify with the standards and assumptions that we find dominating the culture around us. This is one aspect of what the Bible diagnoses as love of the world, or worldliness, though we rarely see it that way or call it by that name.

In the present case, society conceives retirement as a watershed event of great significance, because retirement takes one out of what we call the world of work. Whereas, hitherto, we have labored hard in our trade or profession and been accountable in terms of a system we had no part in creating, now we become our own masters and can set our own agenda. Retirement is seen as an invitation to relax, slackening the pace and thrust of our lives, and as such is envisaged as a wholly good thing. Guaranteed lifelong solvency by our pension or unearned income, we off-load our responsibilities and leave to others the organizing, facilitating, monitoring, and adapting of all the things that it used to be our job to manage.

Thus we view retirement as our warrant for taking it easy across the board and prioritizing self-indulgence for the rest of our lives. Billy Graham has observed from time to time that the word *retire* is not in his Bible; one sees the point he is making, and why he should make a point of making it.

In the churches, there are always some who rejoice when retirement comes, because then they have more time for Christian ministry. Yet the common expectation, undiscussed but unchallenged, is that retirees will not continue the Christian learning and leading that were big in their lives while they were at work. The most that the church will expect of them now is that they will continue to support from the sidelines, as it were, the modes of ministry in which others engage.

In personal terms, this winding down may seem natural enough. Not only has the world pensioned them off; they are starting to feel that their bodies are running out of steam, so that reducing the demands they make of themselves is appropriate self-care. By moving us to think this way, however, Satan undermines, diminishes, and deflates our discipleship, reducing us from laborers in Christ's kingdom to sympathetic spectators, and as such passengers whom the congregation carries by means of the exertions of others.

Still taking their cue from the world around, modern Western churches organize occupations, trips, parties, and so forth for their seniors and make pastoral provision for the shut-ins, but they no longer look to these folks as they do to the rest of the congregation to find, feed, and use their spiritual gifts. In this they behave as though spiritual gifts and ministry skills wither with age. But they don't; what happens, rather, is that they atrophy with disuse.

SENIOR BELIEVERS IN MINISTRY

So eldercare in the churches, while rightly taking account of increasing bodily infirmities among the aging, should at the same time seek to cherish and continue to harness the ministering capacities that these Christians displayed at earlier stages of their lives. And elderly Christians themselves should press on in the worship and service of God, and in pastoral care for others, up to the limit of what they still can handle in terms of learning and leading, as they used to do earlier in their lives.

A word, now, about each of the two activities just mentioned, both of which involve more than is sometimes appreciated.

Learning

Lifelong learning, both of the truths by which Christians are to live and of the way to live by them—also of how these things are taught in Scripture and how they are misstated, misunderstood, and misapplied in the modern world—is every Christian's calling. In former days this enterprise of teaching and learning in the church was labeled *catechesis*, but that word is unfamiliar today, principally because the thing itself is not being done.

The Pastoral Letters in the New Testament all indicate, one way or another, that the church must expect to be constantly infected by misbelief as well as misbehavior. And congregations in every age must see themselves as learning communities in which gospel truth has to be taught, defended, and vindicated against corruptions of it and alternatives to it. Being alert to all aspects of the difference between true and false teaching, and of behavior that expresses the truth as distinct from obscuring it, is vital to the church's health.

It must be said with greatest clarity that alongside devotional Bible study that feeds faith and prompts prayer, something with which most Western Christians are already familiar and in which they are currently engaged, there is equal need of catechetical Bible study, without which well-intentioned minds and hearts will repeatedly go off track, and with which most Western Christians are at present unacquainted.

Leading

It must also be said with equal emphasis that everyone is leader to someone, whether pastoral persons to those they guide and teach, or parents to children, or spouses to each other in complementary ways, or friends to friends. I speak of leadership in a broad sense to include the full reality, informal as well as formal and unconscious as well as intentional, of *influence*: a relational force shaping some aspect of someone else's life. To shrink the idea of leadership so that it only covers institutionalized forms of primacy, as in the armed forces or political parties or business organizations (a shrinkage commonly practiced nowadays) is in my view to ignore its most potent mode.

In close and affectionate relationships there is always an element of leadership, certainly operating one way if not both ways, and thus leadership responsibility becomes a reality that needs to be recognized; for, willy-nilly, we are going to have something of a shaping influence on others, and if we do not impact them for good, we shall be in danger of leading them astray, mal-forming them, as one might say, and who wants that?

Christian wisdom alerts us to be always aware of the reality of influence via intimacy and to seek always to give good leadership to those to whom we are closest. The Bible shows us that this leadership relation may operate intergenerationally (as with Moses and Joshua, or Paul and Timothy) and looks for it to function in family contexts, where fathers and father figures address young men as sons whom they seek to instruct (so in Proverbs and Ecclesiastes).

But to think of Christian retirees as exempt from the twin tasks of learning and leading, just because they do not inhabit the world of wage and salary earning any longer, and for aging Christians to think of themselves in this way, as if they have no more to do now than have fun, is worldliness in a strikingly intense and, be it said, strikingly foolish form.

GOD'S PATH FOR
AGING BELIEVERS

Several times in the New Testament we find the Christian life vividly pictured as running a race. "Let us run with endurance the race that is set before us, looking to Jesus" (Heb. 12:1–2). Similarly, Paul reasons with the undisciplined Corinthians:

> Do you not know that in a race all the runners run, but only one receives the prize? So run that you may obtain it. Every athlete exercises self-control in all things. . . . So I do not run aimlessly; I do not box as one beating the air. But I discipline my body and keep it under control, lest after preaching to others I myself should be disqualified. (1 Cor. 9:24–27)

The apostle's image works by "as if" logic; it calls for running *as if* you were competing and so had to go as fast as you could in order to beat your rivals. Paul uses "run," with these overtones, again in Galatians 2:2 and Philippians 2:16 as an image of his life of serving God. Finally, as an old man (Philemon 9) facing martyrdom, he says: "The time of my departure has come. I have fought the good fight" (the image is probably from wrestling), "I have finished the race, I have kept the faith. Henceforth there is laid up for me the crown of righteousness" (counterpart of the victor's laurel wreath in Greek games) (2 Tim. 4:6–8).

Put positively, the apostle's race image clearly combines these four notions: first, clearheaded goal orientation (you run to win); second, purposeful planning (you think out how you should run the race, pacing yourself and preparing for the final burst); third, resolute concentration (you put everything second to training for and then running and hopefully winning the race); and fourth, supreme effort (you run flat out, putting everything you have got into what you are doing). Thus Paul conceives the faithful Christian life; the believer *runs*, as did he.

Granted, this is not Paul's only perspective on the Christian life. In terms of its theology and the revealed truth that shapes it, it is a life of *gratitude* for grace received, a matter of being moved and motivated by the overwhelming glory of God's redeeming love to a person as naturally unlovable and unacceptable as oneself. "I appeal to you . . . by the mercies of God, to present your bodies as a living sacrifice, holy and acceptable to God, which is your spiritual worship" (Rom. 12:1). And in terms of its temper and the need for steady persistence in it, the Christian life is for Paul a *walk*, a matter of keeping on keeping on along the set path and declining to be distracted from it. "As you received Christ Jesus the Lord, so walk in him, rooted and built up in him and established in the faith, just as you were taught, abounding in thanksgiving" (Col. 2:6–7).

But, as we have just seen, the image of running was central to Paul's understanding of his own life, and I urge now that it ought to be the central focus in the minds and hearts of all aging Christians, who know and feel that their bodies are slowing down. The challenge that faces us is not to let that fact slow us down spiritually, but to cultivate the maximum zeal for the closing phase of our earthly lives.

Why zeal? Because it is zeal that will keep us running. But what is zeal? Rarely do we hear the word or use it ourselves these days, so it is no wonder if we are less than clear as to its meaning. But Nehemiah 3–6 tells us how, against all odds, in fifty-two days Jerusalem's able-bodied inhabitants rebuilt all two miles of the ruined city wall, which is a classic display of zeal in action. And then early in John's Gospel we read of

Jesus cleansing Jerusalem's commercialized temple with awe-inspiring ferocity, and we are told, "His disciples remembered that it was written, 'Zeal for your house will consume me'" (John 2:17, citing Ps. 69:9).

Zeal for his kingdom is a character quality of God himself, as he has revealed himself (Isa. 9:7). So zeal for God's cause, his kingdom, and his glory, all of which the temple symbolized, is one element of the image of God in his incarnate Son—the image in which, so we are told, Christians are to be renewed, and actually are being renewed, by the Holy Spirit (2 Cor. 3:18; Eph. 4:20–24; Col. 3:10). Nowhere does Scripture suggest that this divine renewing process is programmed to go on hold as we age, however true it is that we can clog it up at any point by our own follies and wrong attitudes.

It follows, then, that as zeal for God and godliness and God's honor was integral to

God's image in Christ, so it should be in us, and we should cultivate zeal, along with the rest of Christian virtues, up to the ending of our lives on earth—or at least, for as long as we can consciously focus and direct our thoughts. (As we all know, various kinds of heart failure and dementia, along with the palliative techniques of modern medicine, may involve for us extended spells of comatose or semicomatose existence near the end of earthly life, but these are outside our present concern.)

So again we ask, what is zeal? Zeal means priority, passion, and effort in pursuing God's cause. In the second half of the nineteenth century J. C. Ryle, "the best man in the Church of England," according to the Baptist C. H. Spurgeon, produced the following classic statement on the subject:

> Zeal in religion is a burning desire to please God, to do his will, and to advance

his glory in the world in every possible way. . . .

A zealous man in religion is pre-eminently a man of one thing. It is not enough to say that he is earnest, hearty, uncompromising, thorough-going, whole-hearted, fervent in spirit. He only sees one thing, he cares for one thing, he lives for one thing; and that one thing is to please God. Whether he lives, or whether he dies—whether he has health, or whether he has sickness—whether he is rich, or whether he is poor—whether he pleases man, or whether he gives offense—whether he is thought wise, or whether he is thought foolish—whether he gets blame, or whether he gets praise—whether he gets honour, or whether he gets shame—for all this the zealous man cares nothing at all. He burns for one thing; and that one thing is to please God, and advance God's glory. If he is consumed in the very burning, he cares not for it—he is content. He feels that, like a lamp, he is made to burn; and if consumed in burning, he has but done the work for which God appointed him. Such a one will always find a sphere for his zeal. If he cannot preach, work, and give money, he will cry, and sigh, and pray. If he cannot fight in the valley with Joshua, he will do the work of Moses, Aaron, and Hur, on the hill (Ex. 17:9–13). . . . This is what I mean when I speak of "zeal" in religion. (*Practical Religion* [Cambridge, UK: James Clarke, 1959], 130)

Maintaining zeal Godward as our bodies wear out is the special discipline to which we aging Christians are called. Realism requires us to remember that memory, particularly short-term memory, will weaken; logical tightness of speech will loosen; powers of concentration will diminish; physical exhaustion will overtake us sooner or later, and energy levels will keep going lower. Zeal, however, should be unflagging every day, all day, and all the way. But if this is to happen, zeal must be fed by hope. That is the final point that I have to make, and as was the case before, it too is a theme requiring a chapter to itself.

4

We Look Forward

We humans are hopers by nature. Hope motivates, energizes, and drives us. It is natural to us to look ahead and long for any good things that we foresee. That is how God made us. It was always in his plan that we, his embodied rational creatures, should live our lives in this world looking forward to, and preparing for, something even better than we have known already.

How humanity would have transitioned

into that even better life, had there been no fall into sin, and whether in that case any form of physical wearing out would have preceded the transition are more than we can know. The Old Testament comes to us out of a world in which the originally planned transition has already come to grief through sin and been replaced by a grim reality not known before, namely death, in which self and body are separated. One of the plethora of good things that the New Testament makes known to us, however, is that the essence of this part of God's creational plan has now been restored for us through the death and resurrection of the God-man, Jesus Christ.

But one of the truly sad features of today's secular Western culture, post-Christian as it likes to declare itself to be, is that it has no place for any such hope. Short-term, this-worldly hope—hope of recovering from this or that illness, or disability, or relational or financial setback, and hope of succeeding in this or that enterprise and of avoiding this or that disaster—are familiar to us. But long-term hope, eternal hope as we might call it—hope, that is, that looks beyond this world and extends endlessly—is tied to faith in God, the triune God of Christianity, and as such is something to which our world has become a stranger.

The countries that once called themselves Christendom have drifted away from Christian faith and thus have lost touch with Christian hope. This is a huge loss; for as the New Testament presents the Lord Jesus Christ as fulfilling the divinely promised hopes of Israel, so it presents faith in him as restoring to us the hope of an unimaginably glorious future. There will be an effectual elimination of evil, an endless extrapolation of good, an ecstatic extension of fellowship with the glorified Christ and glorified Christians, and an eternal enjoyment of God's glory and beauty in ways that we cannot at present begin to conceive.

"In this hope we were saved," says Paul, picturing what is coming as total renewal of the cosmos (Rom. 8:24). And Peter unleashes his full resources of rhetoric in celebration of the wonder and joy of it all for persons with faith:

> God . . . has caused us to be born again to a living hope through the resurrection of Jesus Christ from the dead, to an inheritance that is imperishable, undefiled, and unfading, kept in heaven for you, who by God's power are being guarded through faith for a salvation ready to be revealed in the last time. In this you rejoice, though now for a little while, if necessary, you have been grieved by various trials, so that the tested genuineness of your faith—more precious than gold that perishes though it is tested by fire—may be found to result in praise and glory and

honor at the revelation of Jesus Christ. Though you have not seen him, you love him. Though you do not now see him, you believe in him and rejoice with joy that is inexpressible and filled with glory, obtaining the outcome of your faith, the salvation of your souls. (1 Pet. 1:3–9)

The New Testament is full of eager anticipation of the public appearance of Jesus Christ to raise and re-embody all the dead, to renew and reorder the cosmos, and to judge all mankind, taking the faithful to himself and separating from himself those who, whatever role they played in church life, were never truly his, along with those who rejected him from the start.

We cannot survey all this material here, and in any case not all of it is relevant to our present purpose. But I can, and do now, urge that the world-changing impact made by Christians during the first hundred years reflected directly the joy and excitement with which they grasped this hope of glory (or, should I say, with which this hope of glory grasped them). The Roman Empire was a world that, like our world today, lacked any energizing hope of its own, which explains why so many listened hungrily to the Christian message. And I go on to urge that recovering and reappropriating this hope is a prime task for us who are aging today.

WHAT LIES AHEAD

The passage I shall now explore for this purpose is 2 Corinthians 4:16–5:10.

Note first its context and flow of thought. Paul is making an extended apologia to the Corinthians for the apostolic ministry that he fulfills and that they have belittled. Having celebrated his privilege in ministering the gospel of Christ to them, and thereby God's gift of the Holy Spirit, he acknowledges that "we have this treasure in jars of clay" (4:7) and generalizes about his divinely appointed life of affliction (4:8–12). "Our outer self," he says, "is wasting away" (4:16). This theme, of strength being drained by pains and pressures, reappears in 6:3–10, 11:23–29, and in 12:7–10, where Paul speaks of his permanent thorn in the flesh, of which we know only that it was physical (or he would not have said it was in the flesh) and that it was painful (or he would not have called it a thorn).

Paul's aim of restoring his relationship with the Corinthians leads him to show himself to them as the battered apostle—an emphasis that must resonate today with many whose bodies give them increasing trouble (aches, pains, restrictions) as they live through the elongated aging process that modern medical services bestow upon them. This elongation commonly brings increased body-consciousness, by which I mean sustained awareness that our bodies are not all they were and now in effect beg us to go easy in the demands we make on them. Such body-consciousness belongs not in youth, but in old age, when it is not a blessing but a burden. Paul was somewhere in middle life when he wrote 2 Corinthians; one guesses that with the ill treatment he had received, he had aged fast and felt it.

But Paul's spirit was not broken, not even, it seems, bruised, by the state of his battered body. Linking his missionary colleagues with himself, he explains that "we who live are always being given over to death for Jesus' sake, so that the life of Jesus also may be manifested in our mortal flesh" (4:11), and he declares more than once that "we do not lose heart" (4:16; also 4:1; 5:6, 8). The verbs he uses here express cheerful, eager confidence in the face of trouble. And now he moves into a high-flying passage (5:1–10) that grounds this cheerful confidence in four momentous things that "we know" (5:1); that is, four revealed truths.

First revealed truth: We know that a new body awaits each servant of Christ (2 Cor. 5:1). Paul pictures this as a house in heaven, already built by God for us to live in, with our name on it as it were, now awaiting our arrival. The body we inhabit at present is by comparison a tent: a temporary residence, with earth flooring, that may leak and that lacks amenities and will inevitably wear out in a way that the new house will not. Tent-maker Paul knows that living in the new house will be far and away the better option.

Second revealed truth: We know that the experience of moving into this upgraded ac-commodation, our resurrection body, linked as it will be in some way with the body we have now—though as different from it as a seed is from the plant that grows out of it (see 1 Cor. 15:35–49)—will come to us as an enormous enrichment of the embod-ied life as we have known it up till now.

In 2 Corinthians 5:3–4 Paul speaks of this transformational event as an experience not of being stripped or denuded through finishing with our present bodies, but of being "further clothed" (or "clothed upon"), as when, on a cold day, one adds an overcoat to what one is already wearing before venturing out of doors. Paul's somewhat unusual verb expresses this quite precisely. His metaphor is fuzzy at the edges, but clear at the center; it pictures, not the method of our transition from the old body to the new one, but its result.

In the new body we shall be fully comfortable in our new environment ("heaven"—2 Cor. 5:1), just as a person wearing an overcoat is fully comfortable when out in the cold. And in the new body there will be no sense, ever, of reach exceeding grasp, or desire outstripping capacity, or weakness sabotaging strength. Whatever we find ourselves wanting to do we shall discover that we can do. All that is mortal and points to our mortality will have been "swallowed up by life" (5:4). Paul finds this glorious to look forward to, and as our present bodies grow weaker, so, like him, should we. God prepares us for our transforming transition by stirring us up to desire it, and he assures us that it is on its way to us by means of our experience of the Holy Spirit's present supernaturalizing of our lives, whereby we acknowledge the truth about Jesus Christ and come to experience his power (5:5).

Third revealed truth: In heaven, clothed in our new bodies, we shall see and be at home with Jesus our Lord in a way that while we inhabit our present bodies is not possible. And our purpose then, grateful, wholehearted, adoring, and spontaneous, will be to please him, just as for real Christians it is already (5:6–9).

Fourth revealed truth: We, with all other Christians and all other people too, will one day face the judgment seat of Christ. What will be determined then (on resurrection day, presumably) is not where we shall spend eternity—that was decided when we first committed ourselves to Christ and received our forgiveness and reconciliation with God through the cross—but in what condition we shall spend that eternity of life with Christ.

Paul's thought apparently is that the quality of our unending enjoyment of Christ's love and goodness will in some way correspond to the quality of love and devotion to him that marks our lives now (5:10). His reference to knowing "the fear of the Lord" (5:11) then hints at the sad possibility that slackness and irresponsibility in Christ's service now might unfit one for the fullest fullness of heaven's joy. So he takes care not to grow slack in his ministry of evangelistic persuasion.

We see, then, that Paul's knowledge of his hope in Christ had great invigorating, driving, and refreshing force in the very bumpy ride of his peripatetic ministry. We see too that whatever admonitions Paul might have addressed to aging Christians (the New Testament gives us no example of such), recommending relaxation and taking things easy would not have been among them.

WHAT NOW?

One of the staples of folk wisdom everywhere is that, when all is said and done, you have to do the best you can with what you have got. How does this apply to aging Christians like the present writer and his peers? Let us pull together some threads from what we have been saying and try to see.

What have veteran church-linked Christians got as resources to deploy, treasures to share, and wisdom to draw on? Assuming that, though elderly, they remain sound in wind and limb, and free from conscious or unconscious mental disorders, distortions and delusions, do they bring anything unique to the table of Christian fellowship, of kingdom vision, and of disciple-making strategy? Four things touched on earlier call for mention here.

Opportunity

The twenty-first century is a new era for seniors in the Western world, in the sense that today's health services lengthen life and maintain mobility beyond anything that earlier generations ever envisaged. It has become commonplace for seniors to function fairly well right through their eighties and into their nineties. The assumption that was general in my youth, that only a small minority would be fit and active after about seventy, has become a thing of the

past. Churches, society, and seniors themselves are still adjusting to the likelihood
that most Christians who hit seventy still
have before them at least a decade in which
some form of active service for Christ remains practicable.

Maturity

"Ripeness," to use Shakespeare's felicitous
word, develops as does fruit—by a process
of assimilating nutrients and reacting to the
climate: a process that takes its own time
and cannot be hurried. This is as true of
Christlike spiritual maturity as it is of any
other form of human growing. The nutrients in this case are the truths of the Bible
and its gospel; the climatic factors, if I may
put it so, are the aspects of Christian community in church, in family, and in other
human units that have been the Christian's
milieu over the years.

Christian seniors ought to be further

along the path of ripeness than others, but variations of nutrients and climate will affect spiritual growth in significant ways. Spiritual maturity is a deep, well-tested relationship to our triune God through our Lord Jesus Christ, and a quality of relationship with both believers and unbelievers that embraces concern, sympathy, warmth, care, wisdom, insight, discernment, and understanding. It is a quality that is identifiable only in relationships; one that all pastoral ministry requires; and one that should, and in fact constantly does, mark out Christian seniors, equipping them for ongoing usefulness in care-centered, outreach-oriented congregations.

Humility

Pride, that is, self-promotion and self-aggrandizement in disregard of God and at others' expense, has classically been identified as the heart of human sin, as we noted earlier. Humility is the product of ongoing repentance as one decides against, turns from, and by watching and praying seeks to steer clear of pride in all its forms. And as the battle against pride in the heart is lifelong, so humility should become an ever more deeply seated attitude of living at the disposal of God and others—an attitude that veteran Christians should increasingly display. Real spiritual growth is always growth downward, so to speak, into profounder humility, which in healthy souls will become more and more apparent as they age.

Intensity

By this I mean not nervous tension, but strength of focus and concentration on pleasing God and furthering his cause and his glory—in a word, zeal, as we analyzed it a moment ago. Secular society does not expect or encourage any form of zeal among the elderly, but that is just one facet of the world's winding-down ethos for seniors that this book urges Christians of all ages to repudiate.

When one has a sure hope that thrills one's heart, eager anticipation of it, delight in the prospect it opens up, and zeal in pursuing it are natural and should be applauded, not derided. As seniors' powers of body, memory, and creativity grow less, so their conscious focus on their hope of glory should grow sharper and their meditations on it grow more joyful and sustained. As this happens, passion to continue being of use to God and his people, in holiness, love, and what Scriptures conceives as neighborliness, should and will intensify, to the very end.

In this it is important that we should not forget our own families, even if they seem to be forgetting us. In the urban West, the nuclear family (one or two parents, with usually one, two, or three children) has come to be seen as the natural, indeed ideal, human unit, with which grandparents, uncles, aunts, and other seniors should only be loosely linked and to which they will not ordinarily be asked to contribute more than goodwill from a distance and sometimes a spare pair of hands.

For seniors to invade family circles unasked—dictatorial in-laws, for instance, who have not grasped that in life, as in Scripture, loyalty to one's spouse should trump the claims of parents—is undoubtedly unhealthy. But it is also bad for families to ignore mature wisdom that is available to them in the persons of older relatives and friends. Christian seniors should make a point of being available to give as much help of this kind as families are willing to receive, and of showing themselves affectionate, equable, and (if I may coin a word) unsnubbable as they do so. And they should remember that, in any case, the larger need and the wider sphere of ministry to which they should be attending is in the church.

To seniors who, rather than settle for being served by the church but otherwise not counting in its life, have it in them to welcome the opportunity for further serving Christ that their extended health gives them, and who seek to match my threefold anatomizing of the healthy ager's heart, as set out above, I now say: over to you. Ask God, and consult your congregation's pastoral leaders, as to how you might do the best you can with what you have got and model in your own person the mobilizing of over-sixty-fives to continue giving all they can for as long as they can to contribute to the mutual ministry that goes on within God's flock.

As a carer for the needy; a friend and encourager of the lonely and depressed; a companion of the walking wounded, those weakened by bitterness, anger, and hurts that continue to bleed; a helper of sufferers from dementia, Alzheimer's, and all conditions that rob us of the ability to look after ourselves; or as a counselor of those facing marriage, the baptism and upbringing of children, and the strains and crises of family life—each of us who is willing will be found to have a great deal to give for some mode of sympathetic-senior ministry that can in practice be invaluable.

In their book, *A Vision for the Aging Church: Renewing Ministry for and by Seniors* (Downers Grove, IL: IVP Academic, 2011), James Houston and Michael Parker urge that such mobilizing as this can massively enrich churches today, and I close by declaring that I totally agree with them. I hope you do too, and will show it by what you do now.

General Index

Scripture Index

Living the Essentials of the Christian Faith

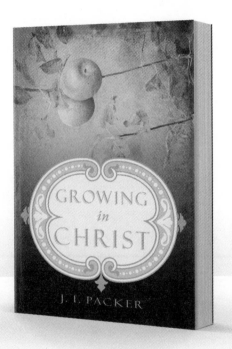

People mature spiritually by learning and living the essentials of the Christian faith. These essentials—so beautifully summarized in the Apostles' Creed, the Lord's Prayer, and the Ten Commandments—provide the heart of this great resource by J. I. Packer that is a must-read for all believers.